YOU CAN MASTER MATH!

Let's Multiply and Divide

By Mike Askew

PowerKiDS press.
New York

Published in 2022 by The Rosen Publishing Group, Inc.
29 East 21st Street, New York, NY 10010

Editors: Ruth Owen and Mark J. Sachner
Designer: Emma Randall

Images courtesy of Ruby Tuesday Books and Shutterstock.

Cataloging-in-Publication Data

Names: Askew, Mike.
Title: Let's multiply and divide / Mike Askew.
Description: New York : PowerKids Press, 2022. | Series: You can master math!
Identifiers: ISBN 9781725331679 (pbk.) | ISBN 9781725331693 (library bound) | ISBN 9781725331686 (6 pack) | ISBN 9781725331709 (ebook)
Subjects: LCSH: Multiplication--Juvenile literature
Classification: LCC QA115.A85 2022 | DDC 513.2'13--dc23

Manufactured in the United States of America

CPSIA Compliance Information: Batch #CSPK22
For Further Information contact Rosen Publishing, New York, New York at 1-800-237-9932.

Contents

Counting with Cookies

Get Ready

You will need:

- Buttons or counters

William and his mom were making cookies. Some cookies had 2 candies on top. Some had 5 candies on top.

William put three cookies on a plate.

"There are two cookies with five candies and one cookie with two candies. That's 12 candies altogether," said William.

"I can make a plate of cookies with 15 candies altogether," said William's mom.

Can you make a plate of cookies with 15 candies? Show how to do it using counters.

What other numbers can you make by adding 5s and 2s?

Are there any numbers you can make in more than one way?

Go For It!

Can you make all the numbers from 20 to 30, using just 5s and 2s?

Five Steps to 100

Get Ready

You will need:
- A die
- Paper and a pen or pencil

In this activity your goal is to get as close to 100 as possible with five rolls of a die. However, you cannot go over 100!

Die roll	Score	Total
Number 1	3	30
Number 2		
Number 3		
Number 4		
Number 5		

1. Roll the die.

   Let's say your score is 3.

2. You can either use the score of 3 or multiply it by 10.
   If you multiply it by 10, that's 30.
   Write down your score.

3. Roll the die a second time.

   Again, decide whether to use the score or multiply it by 10.
   Then add this to your total.

Dice roll	Score	Total
Number 1	3	30
Number 2	6	36
Number 3		
Number 4		
Number 5		

4. Roll the die three more times.

How close did your total get to 100?

Go For It!

Try adding or subtracting your scores. This means if you go over 100, you can subtract a score to get back on track.

Double, Halve, or Stick

Get Ready

You will need:
- A die
- A friend to play with

The aim of this game is for both players to roll the die and work together until one of them makes 25.

1. You can go first. Roll the die and choose whether to:
   Double the number
   Halve the number
   Stick with the number
   ***You can only choose to halve the number if you roll an even number.**
2. Next, your friend rolls the die. They also choose whether to double, halve, or stick with the number shown.
3. Your friend adds their number to your number to make a running total.
4. Keep taking turns. If on a turn the running total is going to go over 25, that player can't go.
5. The winner is the player who hits 25 exactly on their turn!

Here's an example of a game:

Player One: I've rolled 3. I'll double to make 6.

Player Two: I've rolled 5. I'll double to make 10. The running total is 16.

Player One: I've rolled 6. If I double that I'll go over 25, so I'll stick. 16 and 6 is 22.

Player Two: I've rolled 5 so I can't go.

Player One: I've rolled 6. I'll halve it to make 3. 22 and 3 is 25. I win!

Go For It!

Try playing the game with some different target numbers.

Sam's Wheels

Sam works in a bicycle repair shop. Today she is checking all the wheels on the bicycles and tricycles.

How many wheels is that altogether?

Can you find a quick way to count all the wheels?

Sam's Repairs

One morning Sam had to check 23 wheels altogether.

How many bicycles and tricycles might she have checked? Can you find more than one answer?

Domino Odd or Even?

Get Ready

You will need:

- A set of dominoes (remove any dominoes with blank sections)
- Two sheets of paper
- A pen or pencil

Get ready to do this activity by labeling one sheet of paper EVEN and the other ODD.

Place the dominoes facedown on the table.

Turn over one domino and add the two numbers.

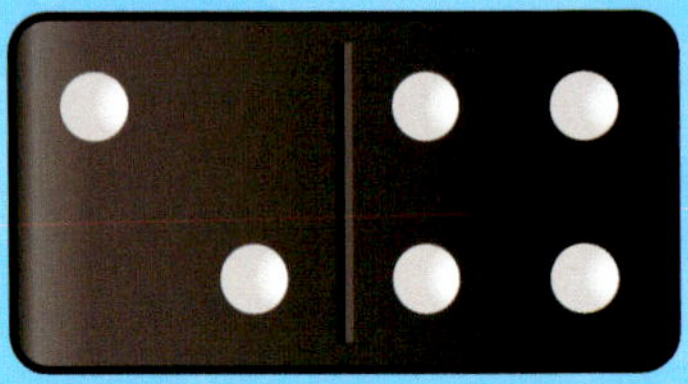

2 + 4 = 6

If the answer is even, put the domino on the paper that's labelled EVEN.

If the answer is ODD, put the domino on the other piece of paper. Sort all the dominoes in this way.

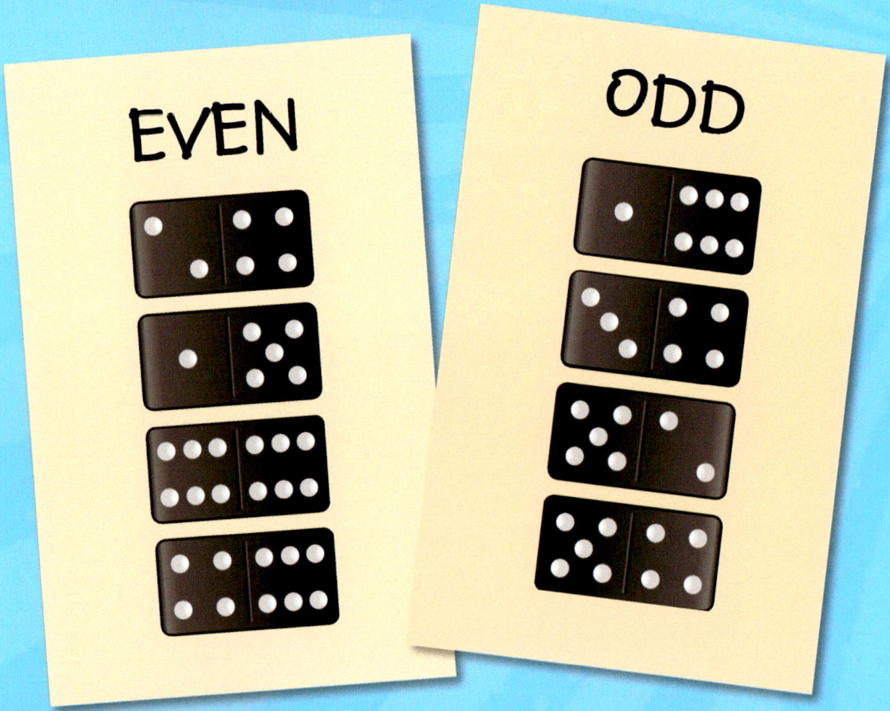

Go For It!

Now look carefully at the dominoes in each group.

What do you notice about the numbers on the dominoes in each set?

Pile 'Em Up

Get Ready

You will need:
- A pack of playing cards
- A die

Play Pile 'Em Up and use a die and cards to become a Master of Multiplication!

1. Roll the die and lay out that number of cards in a row.

2. Roll the die again. The die score is 5. Now add enough cards to each of your 4 piles so that each pile contains 5 cards.

3. Your die scores were 4 and 5. And you now have 4 card piles with 5 cards in each.

   What answer do you get if you multiply 4 by 5?

   Check your answer by counting all the cards you've laid out.

Go For It!

Pick up the cards, roll the die, and go again!

Rock Pool

Look at the rock pool.
The starfish have 5 legs.
The crabs have 10 legs.

Get Ready

You will need:

- A die
- Counters or buttons
- Paper and a pen or pencil

1. Roll the die. Cover that number of starfish with a counter. For example, if you roll 4, put a counter on 4 starfish.
2. Roll the die again. Cover that number of crabs with a counter.

How many legs are there altogether on the starfish and crabs that have counters on them?

Can you show a quick way of working out the total number of legs using your pen and paper?

Go For It!

If there are exactly 60 legs in the rock pool, how many starfish and how many crabs could there be?

How many solutions can you find?

Paper Chains

Get Ready

You will need:

- Lots of strips of colored paper, about 1 inch (2.5 cm) by 6 inches (15 cm)
- A glue stick or sticky tape
- A marker

Let's make a paper chain to show the 3 times table!

1. Take three strips of paper in the same color.
2. Join one strip with glue or tape to make a loop.
3. Thread the second strip through the first loop and join its ends to make two linked loops.
4. Add a third loop. Write 3 on the third loop.

5. Now take three more paper strips in a different color. Add three more loops to your chain. Write 6 on the last loop.

6. Keep adding sets of three loops and label them 9, 12, 15, and so on. Hang up your paper chain of threes.

Go For It!

Make paper chains for the 2, 3, and 5 times tables. Can you make each of the chains the same length? Each chain must end with the same number on it.

Handfuls

Scoop up a handful of counters.
Can you put your counters into
equal groups with none left over?
Each group must contain more than one counter.

Get Ready

You will need:

- Lots of counters or buttons
- Paper and a pen or pencil

For example, you pick up a handful of 15 counters.

Can you put the same counters into groups of a different size?

Remember! There must not be any counters left over.

Now it's your turn!

Scoop up a handful of counters and try putting them into equal groups.

Each time you make a different set of equal groups, give yourself that many points.

For example, if you can divide your counters into 2 equal groups, you get 2 points.

3 groups = 3 points

4 groups = 4 points

And so on . . .

Write down your points. When you can't make any more equal groups, add up your points.

What was your total score for that handful?

Go For It!

Now, try again with a different-sized handful of counters.

Can you beat your last score?

Four in a Row

Get Ready

You will need:

- Counters in two colors
- Two markers (paper clips work well)
- A friend to play with

1. Each player takes a set of counters. The game will be played on the track and board on page 15. The players decide who goes first and that player picks up the two markers (paper clips).

2. Player One puts the markers on the track.

   For example, on 2 and 6:

1	2	3	4	5	6

   If you wish, you can put both markers on the same number.

3. Player One multiplies the two numbers.

4. If the answer is on the board, Player One covers it with a counter.

15	1	8	5	12	2
12	30	2	8	4	6
6	15	18	12	24	20
10	5	15	3	36	4
16	6	20	4	12	3
25	10	24	6	30	9

5. Player Two moves ONE of the markers to a different number on the track. They multiply the two numbers and, if they can, cover that number on the board with a counter.

   (If the number is already covered, the player cannot put a counter on the board.)

6. The players continue taking turns.

   The winner is the player to put four counters in a row on the board – vertically, horizontally, or diagonally!

1	2	3	4	5	6

15	1	8	5	12	2
12	30	2	8	4	6
6	15	18	12	24	20
10	5	15	3	36	4
16	6	20	4	12	3
25	10	24	6	30	9

Card Capers

Get Ready

You will need:

- A pack of cards with the picture cards removed
- A friend to play with

Multiplication Battle

1. Shuffle, or mix up, the cards. Deal the cards equally between the two players.
2. Each player puts their cards facedown in a pile in front of them.
3. Both players turn over their top two cards. Then each player multiplies their two cards together. (Aces count as number 1.)
4. The player with the larger answer keeps all four cards.

5. When all the cards have been turned over, the winner is the player with the most cards.

Player 1

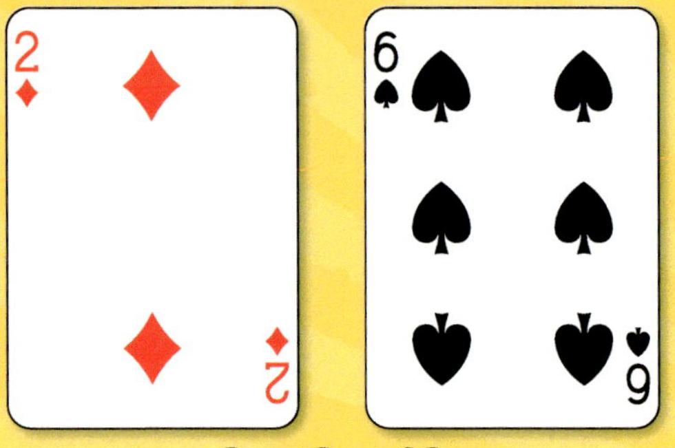

2 x 6 = 12

Player 2

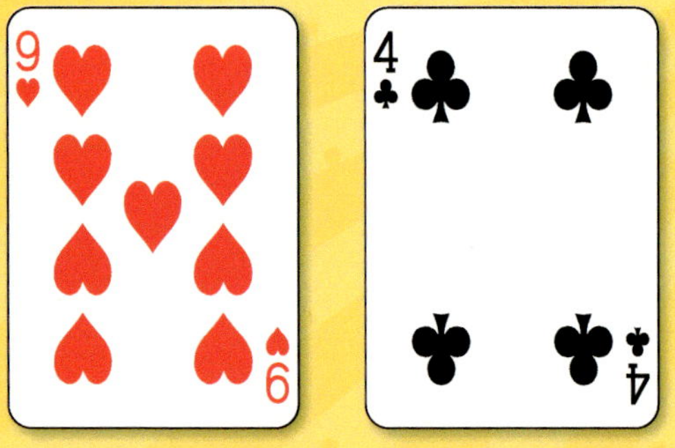

9 x 4 = 36

Go For It!

Try rolling a die before each turn of the cards.

If the die shows an even number, the player with the larger answer wins that round.

If the die shows an odd number, the player with the smaller answer wins that round.

Above or Below Eleven?

Get Ready

You will need:

- A pack of cards with just the numbers 1 to 6 (24 cards in total. Aces count as 1)
- A friend to play with

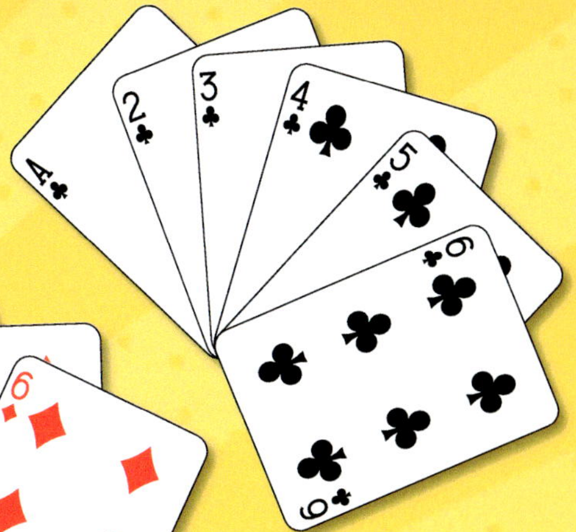

1. Shuffle the cards. Each player gets 12 cards and puts them in a pile, facedown.
2. Player One is trying for less than 11. Player Two is trying for more than 11.
3. Each player turns over their top card. The players now multiply the two numbers together to work out the answer.
4. If the answer is less than 11, Player One collects both cards and puts them to one side. If it's more than 11, Player Two collects both cards.

5. The players keep turning cards over from their original piles and multiplying them. The game is over when all the cards in the players' piles have been turned over. The winner is the player who has won the most cards!

Let's Play EGG-sactly

Get Ready

You will need:

- An empty dozen-egg carton
- A marker
- A marble
- A die

Get ready to play by writing the numbers 1 to 12 in the spaces in your egg carton.

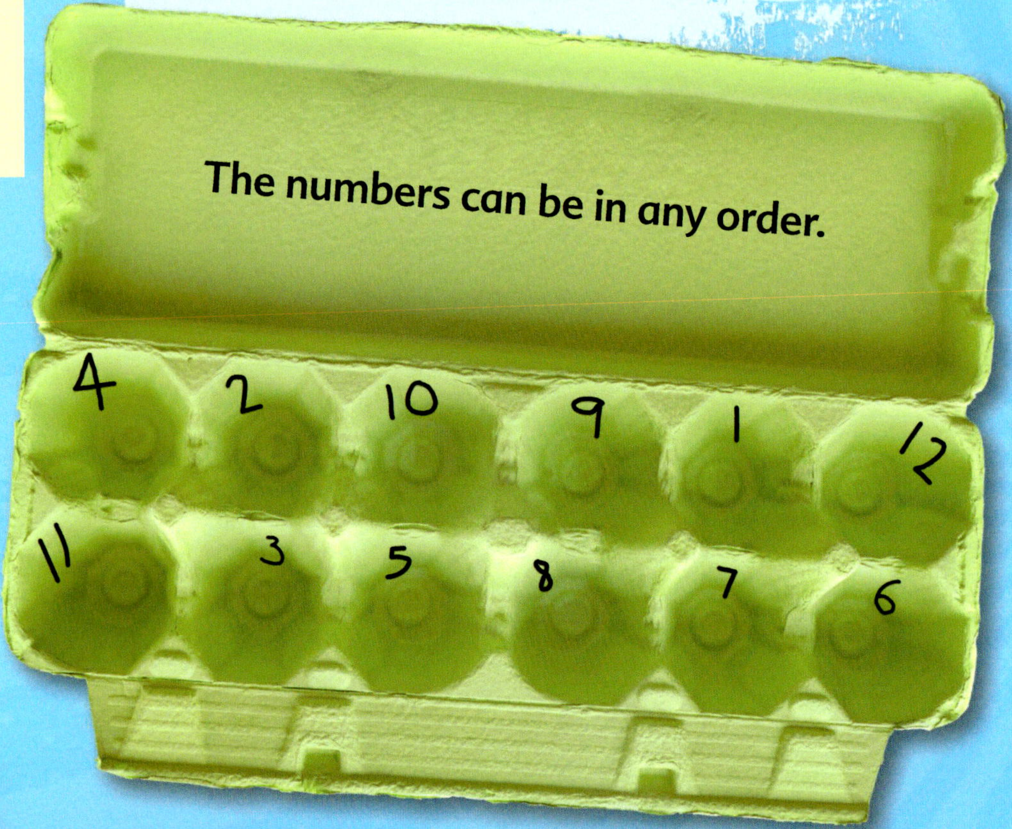

1. Put your marble in the egg carton and close the lid.

2. Roll the die.
3. Shake the egg carton so the marble lands in one of the numbered spaces.
4. Open up the egg carton. Multiply together the number on the die and the number the marble has landed on.

Go For It!

Play EGG-sactly with a friend. The first player to call out the correct answer wins a point. The winner is the first to score 10 points!

Caterpillars

Get Ready

You will need:
- Lots of paper circles
- A pen or pencil
- A glue stick or sticky tape
- Counters or buttons

1. Draw a caterpillar head on a circle of paper. Choose a number between 10 and 20. Write that number on your caterpillar's head. For example, 14.

Take that number of counters.

2. Now halve the number of counters and make two equal groups with none left over. If you choose a number that can't be halved equally, you can add another counter.

Count how many counters are in one group (7 counters). Write that number on a paper circle and stick it to your caterpillar's head.

3. Now take the counters from one of the halves you made and make two equal groups with none left over. If you can't halve the counters equally, you can add another counter.

Count how many counters are in one group (4 counters). Write that number on a paper circle and stick it to your caterpillar.

4. Again, take the counters in one of the halves. If you can halve that number, do so and add it to your caterpillar.

If at any time you cannot halve a number, take another counter.

Keep going until you get to 1.

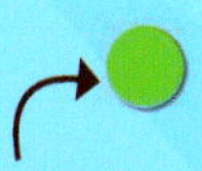

1 counter

Go For It!

Can you find a number between 10 and 20 that will make a longer caterpillar than one that starts with 14?

Get Crafty with 4 and 8

Get Ready

You will need:

- 2 sheets of paper
- Colored pencils or pens
- A glue stick or sticky tape
- Scissors (and an adult to help you with the cutting)

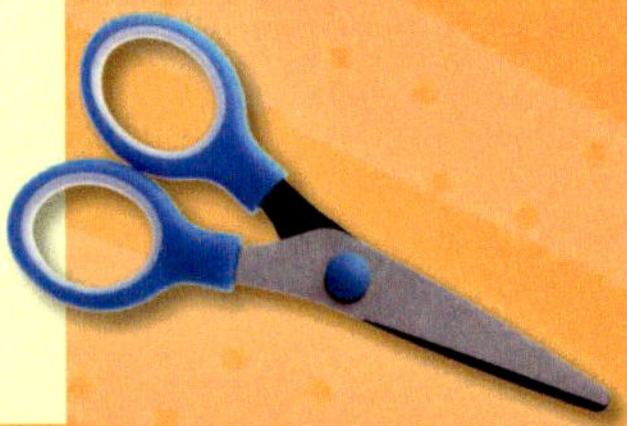

House of 4s

1. On one of the sheets of paper draw a large house with a door and 10 square windows.
2. Write the numbers 1 to 10 on the windows. Write House of 4s on the door.
3. Carefully cut around three sides of each window so they can be opened.

4. Glue your second sheet of paper to the back of the house. Only glue around the edges of the house so your windows will still open.
5. Now open each window and behind it, write down four times the number on the window.

GO FOR IT!

Close all the windows on your house.

Can you say what number is behind each window before you open it up and check?

Flower of 8s

Get Ready

You will need:
- A sheet of paper
- Colored pencils or pens

1. Draw a circle. This is the middle of your flower.

2. Draw 10 petals around the circle. Write the numbers 1 to 10 on the petals.

   The numbers don't have to be in order.

3. Now draw another 10 petals around the outside. In each petal write double the number of the petal that it is next to.

4. Add another 10 petals. Again, in each petal write double the number of the petal it is next to.

5. Finally, add another 10 petals. Once again, write in double the number.

Your flower will look something like this, but the petals will be filled with numbers!

Go For It!

The numbers on the very outside petals are 8 times the numbers in the middle of the flower.

Is what Number 8 says correct?

One, Two . . . Times!

Get Ready

You will need:
- A friend to play with

Each player starts with one hand behind their back.

Take turns to chant:

One, two, times!

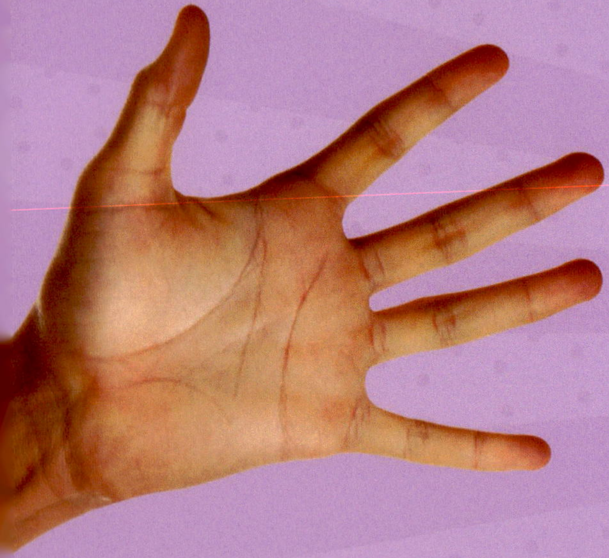

On the word TIMES, each player brings out their hand, showing any number of fingers from zero to five.

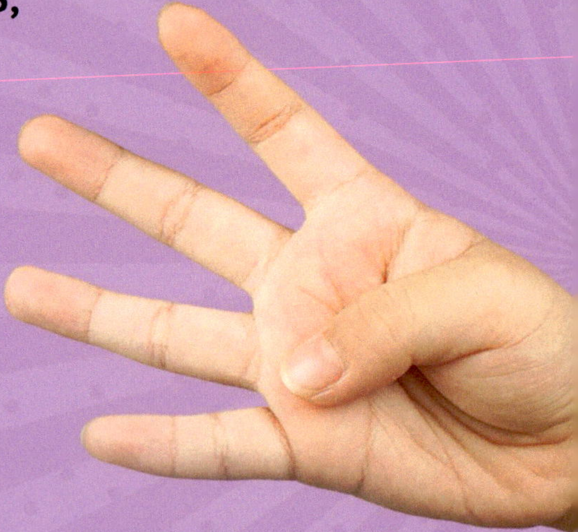

The players must then quickly multiply the two numbers of fingers. The first player to correctly call out the answer scores a point.

Go For It!

Now try with 10 fingers.

The players hide both hands behind their back and on the word TIMES bring out any number of fingers from zero to ten.

Let's Play Darts

Using your counters as darts, what scores can you get on the dartboard?

Get Ready

You will need:
- 3 Counters
- Paper and a pen or pencil

Put three darts (counters) on the dartboard. All three darts must be on the board. More than one dart can be placed in any section on the board.

When you place a dart on the outer ring, the number in the inner ring is doubled or halved.

Go For It!

What is the highest total score you can get by adding up the numbers for each of your three darts? What is the lowest?
Can you find three ways to score 10?
Can you find three ways to score 9?

Mrs. Beaton's Pies

Mrs. Beaton bakes and sells pies. She puts her pies in her shop window in neat rows.

Get Ready

You will need:
- Counters or buttons
- Paper and a pen or pencil

When she bakes 6 pies, Mrs. Beaton likes to arrange them like this:

She doesn't like them arranged like this ...

... or this.

Today, Mrs. Beaton has baked 12 pies.

Take 12 counters. How many ways can you arrange your counters that would please Mrs. Beaton?

Go For It!

How many ways can you arrange 15 counters? How about 20 counters?

What numbers between 10 and 20 could Mrs. Beaton arrange in the most number of ways?

Write down or draw your answers.

Four's Fantastic Facts

Numbers arranged in this way are in arrays.

This is a 2 by 4 array.

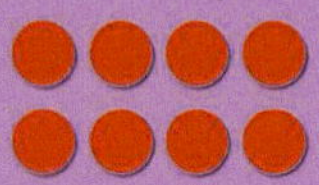

This is a 4 x 2 array.

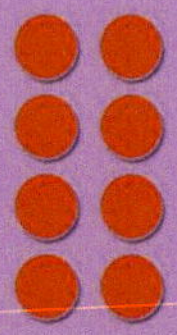

Duck Ponds

Get Ready

You will need:
- Counters or buttons
- Paper and a pen or pencil

In this game, your counters will be the ducks.

Use your counters to put ducks in the four ponds.

Each pond must have either 3 or 4 ducks.

Can you put exactly 14 ducks on the ponds?

Write down your solution.

Is Number 4 correct?

Show on paper how you know this.

Go For It!

Use your counters to put ducks in the four ponds again.

This time, each pond can have either 2 or 5 ducks.

Which of these numbers can you NOT make in the ponds?

8 11 14 15 17 20

Let's Play Cover Up!

You can play Cover Up using the board on page 27.

Get Ready

You will need:

- Two sets of playing cards 1 to 8 (16 cards in total. Aces count as 1)
- Lots of counters or buttons

1. Shuffle the cards and put them facedown in a pile.
2. Turn over the top two cards. Multiply the two numbers together.

   For example:

3 x 4 = 12

3. The answer is 12, so take 12 counters.
4. Now, put the 12 counters on the board in a neat array. For example, you can make arrays like these:

However, the counters cannot be put on the board like this:

These arrangements are not arrays.

5. Now, turn over the next two cards. Multiply the numbers and take that number of counters. Put the counters on the board in another array. For example:

1 x 8 = 8

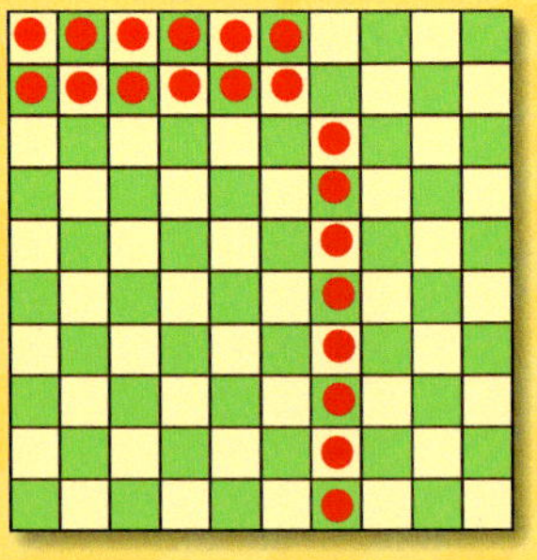

6. Keep turning over and multiplying your cards. When you've used up the whole pile, you can reuse them. The challenge is over when an answer gives you a number of counters that you cannot put on the board as a neat array.
7. Count the squares on the board that are NOT covered by a counter. This is your score.
8. Play again!

   Can you beat your last score by having a smaller number of squares not covered at the end of the game?

Silly Stories

Who can make up the silliest math story problem?

Get Ready

You will need:

- **4 counters**
- **A die**
- **A friend to play with**

1. Roll the die. Use the score to decide who will be the characters in your story. Place a counter next to those characters.

Who

1. Teacher and student
2. Shopkeeper and customer
3. Hare and tortoise
4. Witch and wizard
5. Clown and juggler
6. You and your best friend

2. Roll the die again. Use the score to decide where your story takes place.

Where

1. In the park
2. At the cinema
3. In a car
4. At the top of a tower
5. At the hospital
6. In the kitchen

3. Roll the die again. Use the score to decide what the characters are doing.

What

1. Playing football
2. Knitting a scarf
3. Painting a wall
4. Singing a song
5. Wrapping a present
6. Writing a letter

4. Roll the die again. Use the score to decide what mathematical word or words have to be in your story.

Math Words

1. Times
2. Divided by
3. Shared equally
4. Multiplied together
5. Multiplied by
6. Equal groups

5 Roll the die one last time. The score on the die has to be one of the numbers in your story.

You and your friend now have 2 minutes to each make up a silly story problem. Decide whose story problem was sillier and that person scores a point!

Here is an example of a silly story:

Witch and wizard (roll 4)

In the kitchen (roll 6)

Wrapping a present (roll 5)

Multiplied by (roll 5)

One of the numbers in your story must be 3

Once upon a time, a witch and a wizard were wrapping up a birthday present. They were doing this in the kitchen because the present was a box of multiplying cakes.

"Do you think Harry will like his present?" the witch asked.

"I am sure he will," said the wizard, "especially when the 3 cakes in the box magically get multiplied by 5!"

"How many cakes will that be?" asked the witch.

Do you know the answer?

Tips for Math Success

Page 4: Counting with Cookies

Counting in twos and fives provides a firm foundation to learning the times tables. This activity will help learners practice counting in twos and fives, but will also engage them in problem-solving. If they try to find all the numbers from 20 to 30, help them put their findings in order so that they can look for patterns. For example, they could draw their solutions like this:

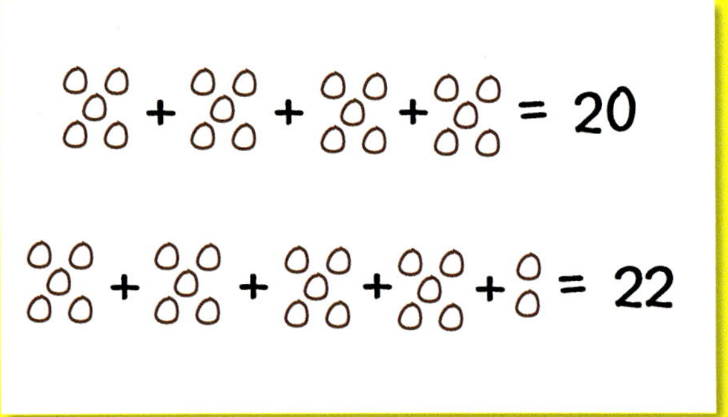

Page 5: Five Steps to 100

Being able to multiply a single number by 10 is a core skill, and this activity provides plenty of practice. When working on multiplying by 10, try not to talk about "adding a zero" (after all, 3 + 0 = 3). Talk instead about a number becoming 10 times bigger.

Page 6: Double, Halve, or Stick

This activity provides practice in doubling and halving, as well as some mental addition.

Page 6: Continued

If learners can double a number, then multiplying by 2 is made easy. So is multiplying by 4 (doubling twice) and by 8 (double again).

For example, 7 times 8 becomes easy!

- doubling 7 is 14
- doubling 14 is 28
- and doubling 28 gives 56

Page 7: Sam's Wheels

Solving this problem will help learners think and work systematically. If they do not spot it, you could point out that since 2 + 3 = 5, it might be quicker to count bicycles and tricycles together (in pairs). This gives a calculation of 8 x 5. There is more than one solution to the 23 wheels problem, so encourage them to continue the search even if they find a solution.

Page 8: Domino Odd or Even?

This game reinforces learners' knowledge of odd and even numbers. Knowing if a number is odd or even helps when halving (dividing by 2). Learners should notice (maybe with a little help) that the dominoes in the EVEN set will all have either two even numbers on them or two odd numbers. The dominoes in the ODD set will all have one odd number and one even number. Help learners notice that adding

Page 8: Continued
two even numbers or two odd numbers will always give an even answer. You can test out this fact using counters.

Page 9: Pile 'Em Up

This simple activity gives learners plenty of practice multiplying numbers 1 to 6. By making piles of cards that relate to the numbers, they also get a tangible example of each calculation that they can use to check their answers.

Page 10: Rock Pool

This activity will give learners plenty of practice multiplying fives and tens.

Page 11: Paper Chains

Many learners benefit from a strong physical sense of the multiplication facts: making a paper chain can help them see where the pattern of 3, 6, 9 and so on comes from. If they go for the challenge, the first number where all three times tables will match up as sets of loops is 30 (15 x 2, 10 x 3, 6 x 5). So the three paper chains will each need 30 links.

Pages 12–13: Handfuls

Obtaining a strong sense of sharing things out into equal groups is the basis of understanding division. Although it's not explicit in this activity, the sorting of counters into equal groups lays the foundation for later work on factors:

15 is 1 x 15 and 3 x 5

So the factors of 15 are 1, 3, 5, 15

12 is 1 x 12, 2 x 6 and 3 x 4

So the factors of 12 are 1, 2, 3, 4, 6, 12

Pages 14–15: Four in a Row

This game provides practice in multiplying and dividing. It also involves strategic thinking as players not only have to try and create their own line of four, but also try to block their opponent.

Pages 16–17: Card Capers

These two card games are easy to set up and give learners plenty of multiplication practice.

When playing "Multiplication Battle," the cards used can be adapted to suit learners' current abilities. For example, if they're not yet confident at multiplying numbers above 6, just play with the numbers 1 to 6.

Page 18: Let's Play EGG-sactly

This game is good fun and a great way for learners to practice all the times tables up to 12.

Page 19: Caterpillars

This activity offers more consolidation of halving numbers. It also provides an opportunity to talk to learners about remainders – the one left over when trying to halve an odd number.

Pages 20–21: Get Crafty with 4 and 8

These fun craft projects will reinforce the 4 times table and help learners understand the relationship between repeatedly doubling and multiplying by 8.

Page 22: One, Two ... Times!

This multiplication game is a variation on rock, paper, scissors. There's no set-up required and it's a great game for long journeys!

Page 23: Let's Play Darts

As well as providing further practice in doubling and halving, this activity will also encourage learners to work systematically.

The lowest score you can get is 3 and the highest score is 30.

Ask learners to find out how many of the numbers between 3 and 18 they can score with their three darts.

Page 24: Mrs. Beaton's Pies

The array is a core idea in multiplication and division. Each column must contain the same number of objects as the other columns and each row must have the same number as the other rows. The power of the array is that it will help learners see why 3 x 4 = 4 x 3. These two calculations are the same array simply rotated through a quarter turn.

If learners try the 10 to 20 challenge, they should find that the numbers 12, 18, and 20 can each be arranged in 6 different arrays.

1 x 12   12 x 1   2 x 6   6 x 2   3 x 4   4 x 3

1 x 18   18 x 1   2 x 9   9 x 2   3 x 6   6 x 3

1 x 20   20 x 1   2 x 10   10 x 2   4 x 5   5 x 4

Page 25: Duck Ponds

These puzzles give learners plenty of practice at dividing a collection of counters into groups of 3 and 4, or 2 and 5.

The numbers 8, 11, 14 , 17, and 20 can all be made with groups of 2 and 5 counters. The number 15 cannot be made.

Pages 26–27: Let's Play Cover Up!

This solo game provides practice in all the multiplication facts from 1 x 1 to 8 x 8. It also involves some strategic thinking, as learners must make careful choices about how to fill up the game board.

Pages 28–29: Silly Stories

Being able to carry out calculations is important. However, learners also need to know when a calculation might be used. They should also be able to confidently use the different terms for multiplication and division. This activity provides a lighthearted way to play with both of these skills.